Original title:
Purpose: Somewhere in the Universe

Copyright © 2025 Creative Arts Management OÜ
All rights reserved.

Author: Elias Marchant
ISBN HARDBACK: 978-1-80566-291-4
ISBN PAPERBACK: 978-1-80566-586-1

Chasing Celestial Echoes

In the dark, we seek a sign,
I tripped over a star line.
"Hey, is that a cosmic joke?"
The moon replied, "No, just smoke!"

Planets spin in silly dance,
Caught in a gravitational trance.
Saturn wears its rings with glee,
While Venus giggles, 'Look at me!'

The Unseen Tapestry

Awe and wonder in the loom,
Weaving threads of cosmic bloom.
A comet sneezes, stars take flight,
"I didn't see a thing!"—a blight.

Galaxies spin, a feathery plight,
While black holes snack on starlight.
They laugh as they twist and spin,
Chasing shadows, let the games begin!

Dance of Celestial Bodies

Stars tap-dance on the night sky,
While asteroids laugh and fly by.
Mars goes wild with disco lights,
"Is that the Milky Way?" —what a sight!

Nebulas swirl in cotton candy,
As aliens host a party so dandy.
They toast with meteorite juice,
While the cosmos laughs with their raucous use!

Sparks of Infinity

Twinkling lights across the gloom,
Each one boasts its own little boom.
"Bet you can't catch a falling star!"
"Oh, please! I'll just call my car!"

Laughter echoes in space's grace,
As atoms join in the crazy race.
Infinite jokes we all can share,
As we float in this cosmic air!

The Thread that Binds the Stars

In a galaxy far and wide,
Stars gossip and twinkle with pride.
They play hide and seek under the moon,
While aliens dance to a funky tune.

Comets get lost, but that's okay,
They just make a wish and fly away.
Nebulas giggle in colors so bright,
Playing tag with the black hole at night.

Beyond the Horizon of Knowing

There's a planet where cows can float,
And chickens wear hats and take a boat.
They debate why the sky is so blue,
While sipping stardust in a cosmic brew.

Rockets run on jellybeans and cheer,
As astronauts laugh without any fear.
They tickle the cosmos with shoots of light,
And dance with the gravity like it's a kite.

A Cosmic Pilgrimage

Martians wear flip-flops and shades in the sun,
While Saturn shows off its rings for fun.
Pluto's the jokester, always a hit,
Telling tales of why he was never a bit.

Asteroids rolling like pinballs in space,
Crack jokes that bring a laugh to every place.
With every twist in the galaxy wide,
They find joy in the cosmic ride.

Whispers of the Ancient Cosmos

The stars have secrets, they chuckle and sway,
With tales of comets that wandered astray.
Galaxies gossip in twinkling delight,
As they plan a party to last through the night.

Black holes are just lazy, they say with a grin,
Clogging the dance floor, it's hard to get in.
But who needs space when you've got a laugh?
In the universe, joy's the best path.

An Interstellar Quest

A spaceship made of tin and dreams,
Zooming past with silly beams.
Aliens wave with goofy grins,
Counting each other's wobbly chins.

Through asteroid fields of candy corn,
Dodging comets that look forlorn.
Whispers from stars, 'What is your aim?'
We yell back, 'Just playing the game!'

In this vastness filled with jest,
We laugh at the universe's wild quest.
With donut-shaped planets on the way,
We dance in orbits, come what may.

Fragments of Eternity

Pieces of stardust in a jar,
Trading them like bizarre bazaar.
A luminescent flea jumps high,
Screaming 'Catch me if you can!' oh my.

Quasars blink in rhythmic tune,
While space whales float past the moon.
Winks from black holes, oh what a sight,
'Wish we could fit, but this couch is tight!'

In this cosmic game of catch and flee,
Joy spread out like a galaxy spree.
Each moment's a chuckle wrapped in light,
Unraveling giggles from day to night.

The Call of Celestial Mist

A comet sneezed and off it flew,
Leaving trails of sparkly goo.
Jupiter grinned, a big ol' tease,
'Breathe in that mist, it's sure to please!'

With asteroids jiving to the beat,
A dance-off in zero gravity, neat!
Silly aliens flash their bling,
Singing loud, 'Oh, let us swing!'

Stars sprinkle laughter in their glow,
Cheering for a cosmic show.
In the mist, we find our cheer,
Silly moments, drawing us near.

Reflections in the Cosmic Ocean

Ripples in space like a wobbly pond,
Reflecting dreams that float just beyond.
Galactic fish with googly eyes,
Nibbling on stardust pies.

With bubbles that giggle and pop,
In this ocean, we'll never stop.
Swimming with joy while we chat,
'Is that a spaceship or a flying cat?'

In remixed rhythms of the light,
We laugh together through the night.
Each wave holds a tale to tell,
In this vast ocean, we all dwell.

Between Celestrial Bodies

In the space between planets, they share a snack,
Saturn's rings wobble, can't hold the pack.
Jupiter's moon laughs, with ice cream in hand,
While comets are trailing a wild, messy band.

Stars keep on twinkling, a competitive lot,
Saying, 'I'm brighter!' as if they forgot.
Black holes are grinning, pulling jokes that are deep,
While galaxies giggle, in the dark, they all sleep.

Echoes of Lost Civilizations

Once there were folks who built pyramids tall,
Now their sneezes echo, a cosmic sprawl.
Alien cultures exchange silly memes,
While Earthlings just dream of their interstellar schemes.

Ancient ruins whisper in giggles and sighs,
As stardust confetti falls from the skies.
They debate on the best way to rule a whole star,
But end up just spinning in circles, bizarre!

A Starry Tapestry Unraveled

In the cosmic quilt, a thread starts to fray,
"Did you pull that?" asked Lyra, "Not me, I say!"
Orion just chuckles, amused by the plight,
While a nebula winks, tucked away in the night.

Strings intertwine in a puzzled mess,
Making starry patterns that add to the stress.
But laughter erupts, it's all just for fun,
As the universe plays fetch with the light from the sun.

Cosmic Dreams and Celestial Schemes

Starships are plotting a galactic rave,
While meteors practice for their jump with a wave.
Uranus just snickers, it's quite a sight,
When planets get dancing under the moonlight.

Eclipses are hiding, a shy little phase,
Watching the chaos, a starlit display.
While quasars are shouting, "We're here to perform!"
Creating a circus, way out of norm!

Celestial Choreography: Dance of Intent

In the vastness, stars take a spin,
Orion's belt always losing its pin.
The moon eats cheese on a plate so wide,
While planets play tag, it's quite a ride.

Saturn wears rings that are fabulous,
While Mars just struts, looking fabulous.
Galaxies twirl in a cosmic ballet,
Laughing at comets that zoom and sway.

The Hidden Significance of Nightfall

Night falls softly, like a cat's gentle pounce,
Whispers of constellations that dance and flounce.
A shooting star tells jokes in the dark,
But the punchline's often lost, just a spark.

While owls wink and give a wise old nod,
The sky's a circus, isn't it odd?
Clouds play hide and seek with the moon,
A celestial game, oh so opportune.

Finding Meaning in Stellar Silence

In silence, the cosmos hums a tune,
Comets giggle under a watchful moon.
Stars whisper secrets between their twinkles,
While black holes just suck and give sly crinkles.

Nebulas giggle, all fluffy and bright,
Creating new worlds out of sheer delight.
With laughter and mischief in stellar disguise,
They ponder the question, 'What's with all these eyes?'

Beneath the Infinite Sky

Under a blanket of twinkling delight,
Aliens debate if frogs are just right.
Asteroids tumble like clowns at a fair,
While satellites float like they haven't a care.

The sun takes a snooze, dreaming of heat,
While space-time giggles, oh what a treat!
In this cosmic circus, we all have a role,
Even the dark void has its sense of soul.

The Heartbeat of Nebulas

In the dance of gas and light,
Stars twirl, trying to get it right.
Cosmic balloons puff and sway,
While comets join the cabaret.

Planets play hide and seek,
Meteors glance, but never peek.
Black holes munch with glee and cheer,
'Who needs a diet? We're out here!'

Among the Starlit Dreams

Asteroids rock to a galactic beat,
Space dogs chase shiny treats.
Aliens laugh with bubblegum sound,
While Saturn's rings spin round and round.

Jupiter bakes a giant pie,
Venus winks, oh my, oh my!
Mars wears red socks, quite the look,
While Earth hides behind a storybook.

The Light Between Worlds

Light sabers clash in a comet's tail,
While worms do the tango in a glowing trail.
Galaxies giggle, what a sight,
As quasars wink through the infinite night.

Stars play tag in a cosmic race,
While cosmic dust gives stars a face.
Nebulae whisper their dazzling schemes,
Wondering if they're stuck in dreams.

Seeking Signs in Dark Matter

Dark matter's hiding, what a joke,
It's just a shy particle playing smoke.
Invisible friends dance in the dark,
While physicists ponder and try to spark.

They look for signals, but all they find,
Are cosmic hiccups that blow their mind.
In the vastness, they laugh and play,
"Maybe dark matter just wants a say?"

Harmonies Among the Heavens

In a galaxy where stars do dance,
Planets gossip, given half a chance.
Meteorites throw a wild party glare,
While comets braid their luminous hair.

The Milky Way says, "Hey, what's that?"
Jupiter ridicules a passing bat.
Black holes suck in laughter and light,
As aliens chuckle at their own flight.

Shooting stars wink with a playful twist,
Whispering secrets that none could resist.
While space dust tickles celestial chins,
Galactic fun never truly begins.

Saturn spins rings, confused with a bling,
In cosmic chaos, all the critters sing.
From distant worlds, they sound a bright note,
In harmonies where nothing's remote.

Celestial Trails in the Night

A starship sails through a sea of dreams,
Little green beings plotting in teams.
They trade odd hats that wobble and sway,
In the great cosmic cabaret ballet.

Satellite snacks float around in glee,
As cosmic cats chase comets just to be free.
Black holes giggle, playing peek-a-boo,
While quasars cheer for the otherworldly crew.

Galaxy hopscotch, who will win this round?
With starry high-fives, they leap off the ground.
Asteroids scramble, avoiding the fate,
Of being a spaceball on a wild date.

In the velvet dark, laughter echoes wide,
Between constellations, where wishes abide.
With cosmic jokes that no one can find,
The trails in the night are splendidly blind.

Celestial Enigmas

Mars wore a hat, looking quite absurd,
While Venus danced, speaking not a word.
The moons all giggled, winked at the sun,
In the game of celestial 'Who's Number One?'

The nebulae swirling, like clouds of cotton,
Wondered out loud if anyone got rotten.
Planets debated who had the best flair,
As Saturn tossed sparkles into the air.

Cosmic riddles spun faster than light,
As ghosts of stardust rose up for a bite.
They sipped on the brew of old cosmic tales,
While orbits laughed at the interstellar fails.

In a riddle maze where the laughter grows,
The motion of planets in dizzying flows,
Unraveled the secrets lost in the void,
Where mysteries dance, giggling and coyed.

Navigation through Cosmic Depths

Navigating stars with a map made of cheese,
Galactic mice munch while floating with ease.
They steer with their whiskers, a spacecraft unbound,
Chasing moonbeams as silly jokes abound.

Asteroids tumble like clumsy old fools,
Avoiding the black hole, a pit full of pools.
Space bunnies hop, taking turns in the air,
With carrots of light, they don't have a care.

Pluto, the underdog, tells silly tales,
Of wandering stars on their feathered sails.
With every light-year, laughter ignites,
In the cosmic circus, where joy takes flight.

So raise up your glasses of starlight and cheer,
For cosmic navigation, there's nothing to fear.
In the depths of the night, may comedy reign,
As the universe pranks us again and again.

Celestial Threads of Intent

In the vastness above, there's a plan,
Stars stitching the sky, yes they can!
Little comets zoom, like they're late to a show,
While black holes gulp down all the dough.

Meteors dance, wearing shiny tails,
Finding their rhythm in cosmic trails.
Asteroids grumble, 'Where's our guide?'
While planets giggle, caught in the ride.

Nebulas puff their pastel hues,
Yelling, 'We're here, don't miss our cues!'
Galaxies spin in a dizzy delight,
Making sure that chaos feels right.

So let's toast to the night's funny scheme,
Where cosmic chaos is the ultimate dream!
Raise your glass to the twinkling sparks,
For in the universe, we're all just larks.

The Whisper of Stardust Dreams

Whispers of stardust float on by,
Tickling the cosmos, oh my, oh my!
Planets gossip in their serene dance,
While meteors crash, dreaming of romance.

A sunbeam sighs, 'Don't take it slow,'
While moons wink, putting on a show.
Saturn's rings jingle, 'Ain't we grand?'
As comets swoosh, like a quick band.

Stars believe they were born to tease,
Hoping to make the night sky please.
Constellations chuckle, drawing their jokes,
From the vibrant clouds of forgotten folks.

So here's to laughter in endless space,
Where every quasar has its own face!
As we drift on waves of celestial whim,
Let's spin our tales on a cosmic rim.

Echoes in the Cosmic Waters

In cosmic waters, bubbles rise,
Reflections of laughter splash in the skies.
Galaxies ripple, tickling the void,
While starlight dances, never destroyed.

Fish with antennae and stars as fins,
Swim through the milky way, grinning grins.
A tidal wave of giggles and cheer,
Filling the universe with joy, never fear.

The constellations mime, oh what a sight,
Pretending to battle in the depths of night.
Neutron stars twist in playful delight,
As cosmic echoes resound in the light.

So, pluck a star, give it a toss,
Who knows, it might just become the boss!
In this galactic whirl, we'll sing and hum,
For every wave of joy's a tune to come.

Navigating the Nebula of Being

In the nebula's haze, we wander and roam,
With glittering thoughts, we navigate home.
Stars wave their arms as if to say,
'Come join our cosmic cabaret today!'

A quirky quasar waves from afar,
Saying, 'Flip a coin, you're a new star!'
With nebula fluff for a comfy seat,
We bounce along to the beat of the tweet.

Galactic maps are just doodles in space,
As planets collide in a jovial race.
What's life without a leap and a dash?
With each stellar trip, we truly make a splash.

So float on joy through the glittering night,
For chaos is fun if you hold on tight!
In the universe's dance, join the spree,
And laugh at the stars, just you and me.

As the Planets Align

In the cosmic circus, planets play,
Juggling orbs in a funny ballet.
Saturn trips on his shiny rings,
While Venus sends hugs with her flinging wings.

Mars stumbles and giggles in red,
Echoes of stardust swirl in his head.
Neptune winks with a splashy grin,
While comets are laughing, and stars spin in.

The Milky Way claps as a supernova cracks,
Black holes chuckling at the light that lacks.
The sun snickers softly, a fiery ball,
As asteroids groove in a cosmic hall.

So when the planets align in a row,
Expect a show that steals the glow.
With stars on stage and laughter so wide,
Join the universe's hilarious ride!

In Search of What Connects Us

A spaceship flies with donuts in hand,
Searching for friends in a quirky band.
Shooting stars giggle at oddball dreams,
While aliens dance in the milky streams.

Backwards comets whizz past my head,
Whispering secrets that I seldom read.
Asteroids argue about who's the best,
While Saturn gets lost in a game of chess.

With laughter like echoes from faraway lands,
Galaxies giggle, weaving their strands.
Through cosmic confetti, we find our crew,
Making connections with a smile or two.

So here we float, silly and free,
In a universe filled with absurdity.
Grinning at life as we chase the sun,
Searching for kin — oh, this is fun!

The Unfolding of Stars

Stars pop out like popcorn at night,
Some twinkle softly, others are bright.
Asteroids catch the latest gossip,
As they tumble and twist on a cosmic trip.

Planets stretch, doing their yoga poses,
Wishing for petals, instead of roses.
Uranus giggles when no one's around,
He's the prankster, a comedic sound.

The stars unfold, and oh what a sight!
Meteor showers turning laughter to light.
A nebula shapes into a silly face,
As the cosmos spins in a merry place.

With cosmic adventures, never a bore,
Infinite moments to giggle and roar.
The universe dances in its silly suits,
Where laughter and stardust are ever in roots.

The Search for Celestial Kin

In the cosmic cafe, we sip on some beams,
Chatting with moons about wildest dreams.
Jupiter's jokes are a blast from the past,
While Martians tell tales of their wild cast.

Galaxies swirl in a disco of light,
With aliens twirling through the starry night.
Comets join in, with slippery slides,
Creating a mess where laughter abides.

So we search for kin in this galactic mess,
Finding connections that leave us impressed.
With our cosmic pals, we create a song,
In the universe's laughter, we forever belong.

So smile big, let the stardust shine,
In a playful dance through the vast divine.
Together we'll giggle, fumble, and spin,
Embracing the joy of inviting our kin!

Journey to the Edge of Infinity

I'm packing my snacks for a trip to the stars,
With twinkling lights and bright, bubbly cars.
I'll wear my best socks, no one will see,
As I float through the cosmos, just sipping my tea.

I asked my spaceship, "Do you want to dance?"
It said, "Only if you give me a chance!"
So we twirled through the Milky Way, side by side,
Leaving behind all our worries and pride.

The aliens laughed, they thought it a show,
As I tripped on a comet and said, "Here we go!"
They offered me snacks, I said, "What a treat!"
I shared my fine biscuits, they thought they were sweet.

We played hide and seek with a supernova blast,
I won by a light year, who knew it was fast?
But then I got lost, in a galactic maze,
The map said, "Turn left, but who's counting days?"

With laughter echoing in the vastness so wide,
I knew I had friends who enjoyed the ride.
We danced among stars, under shimmering light,
In the goofy grand scheme, everything felt right.

The Quest for Celestial Essence

In the void, a chicken flies,
With a spaceship made of fries.
Searching for cosmic snacks to munch,
In a galaxy where aliens lunch.

With a bubblegum comet in its sight,
It dances in the radiant light.
Stars wink as if to say,
"Join us for an interstellar play!"

On a space surfboard, it glides,
Past planets that giggle and slide.
"What's the secret to life?" it asks,
They reply with jokes, in silly masks.

Finally, it lands on a pie-shaped moon,
Where gravity holds a lively tune.
With laughter echoing through the sky,
The chicken feasts, oh my, oh my!

Signposts in the Dark

Under a sky of shimmering hue,
A lost sock searches for its shoe.
It asks the stars for directions clear,
"Are you a guide, or just a big sphere?"

A comet zooms by, with a coffee cup,
"Hang tight, buddy! Let's fill you up!"
With caffeine boosts, they soar and dash,
Through the Milky Way and back in a flash.

They reach a black hole, quite the sight,
Where the universe dances at night.
But the sock just wants to hitch a ride,
To find its partner, in cosmic pride.

In the vastness, they twirl and spin,
A duo of drift, let the fun begin!
With giggles and spins, they break the dark,
Creating twinkling memories, oh what a lark!

Riddles of the Cosmos

Why did the moon blush, tell me please?
It saw an asteroid in a dress of cheese!
Dancing in circles, laughing with stars,
  Chasing comets in their shiny cars.

A galaxy whispers, "What's the big plan?"
  As a sunflower floats by in a can.
Planets giggle, "Let's play hide and seek!"
While a supernova plays peek-a-boo chic.

  A star let out a stream of confetti,
While chasing a nebula, twinkling and petty.
The great cosmic jester swings from above,
  As everyone joins in, oh what a love!

The universe chuckles, with glee abound,
In this cosmic carnival, joy can be found.
With mysteries tickling our curious brains,
Each riddle a spark, where laughter reigns!

Constellations of the Heart

In the sky, a bear and a sheep,
Belly laughing while counting sheep.
"Is this love?" the bear does say,
As the sheep rolls over, donning a bouquet.

Stars twinkle of hearts and silly dreams,
Where unicorns dance at the light beams.
A big dipper filled with honeyed glee,
Served up with cosmic tea, oh what a spree!

Orion is lost, with his belt undone,
As he trips on the stardust, oh what fun!
"Hold my drink," he shouts with flair,
As Venus giggles and twists her hair.

In this celestial realm of light-hearted cheer,
Every heartbeat sings, every laugh sincere.
With constellations crafting tales of delight,
The universe smiles, shining so bright!

The Journey of Cosmic Wanderers

In a ship made of cheese, we sail through the night,
With aliens dancing, oh what a sight!
Gargling with stars, we sip cosmic tea,
Laughing at quasars, just you and me.

Asteroids bounce like rubbery bugs,
Planets in pajamas, sharing warm hugs.
At every stop, there's a galactic fair,
Selling green donuts, without a care.

We traded some stardust for glittery hats,
And danced with the comets, oh what acrobats!
In the vacuum of space, we played hide and seek,
While black holes giggled, they're such little freaks.

As we wander the cosmos, no map to unfurl,
We'll tickle a supernova, give it a whirl!
Forever exploring, this wild carnival,
With friends made of gases, we'll have a ball!

Celestial Reflections

In mirrors of starlight, we comb through the past,
Finding sock puppets in a nebula cast.
Galaxies twirl in a cosmic ballet,
While meteors giggle, saying, "Come play!"

Sipping on moonbeams, dreams light as air,
We ride on the tails of a comet, oh dare!
Mars tells a joke about Saturn's tight rings,
While Jupiter juggles, oh look at his swings!

Dancing with gravity, we float and we swirl,
Every hop brings a cosmic whirl.
From quasars to asteroids, we find our way,
Chasing the giggles through night and through day.

And when twilight falls, with laughter we glance,
At the winking of planets, all ready to dance.
In this infinite mirror, full of delight,
We find all the hope among shadows of light!

Fragments of an Eternal Map

A map made of giggles, with paths drawn in jest,
Leads us to places the brave and the blessed.
With every wrong turn, we find hidden charms,
In suns that make sandwiches and moons with warm arms.

Through high gravity zones, we stumble and bounce,
Past aliens yelling, "Hey, come join the pounce!"
Eclipses with parties, confetti in space,
Floating on wishes, we dance in our place.

Galactic GPS? Nah, we're on our own,
Each star is a guide, we've happily flown.
From wormholes to whirlpools, we twist and we spin,
Collecting odd trinkets, a cosmic win-win!

With laughter as our compass, we venture afar,
Finding joy in the journey, that's our guiding star.
No map leads us wrong when we find joy in claps,
For fragments of laughter are our cosmic maps!

Starbound Serendipity

In the realm of the quirky, where laughter ignites,
We tripped over stardust and danced through the nights.
Astrological ice cream cones swirl in our view,
With sprinkles of laughter and a starry sky blue.

Wormholes as shortcuts to beaches with sun,
Playing fetch with the comets, oh isn't this fun?
Galaxies giggle, tickled by light,
With echoes of chuckles that bounce through the night.

On a rollercoaster made of sparkling dreams,
We whirl through the cosmos on fantastical beams.
In the shade of a planet that's cozy and round,
We'll share goofy stories, all fortune and sound.

So grab your space buddy, let's sail through the stars,
With laughter our fuel, let's travel near, far!
For in this grand journey, with joy we abide,
Starbound serendipity, our cosmic ride!

Interstellar Journeys of the Mind

Through dusty trails, thoughts zoom by,
Chasing meteors with a sigh.
Coffee cups orbit, like moons they flow,
In this vast void, where wild ideas grow.

Space snacks floating, what a delight,
Astro-burgers served in the night.
Planets smile, while comets dance,
In the galaxy's zany expanse.

Plot twist: aliens steal our fries,
While we drift among starlit skies.
Eureka moments spark like gas,
Galaxy-sized laughter, oh what a blast!

In zero-gravity, thoughts take flight,
Bouncing ideas till morning light.
The cosmos sings a quirky tune,
As we scribble dreams on the face of the moon.

Whispers from the Abyss Above

In the dark, stars giggle and glow,
Telling secrets only night owls know.
A shout-out from Jupiter, "Hey, howdy!"
While Earth spins by all blurry and rowdy.

Black holes burp, causing a stir,
As cosmic clowns prance without demur.
"Whoops, there goes the last slice of pie,"
Stars chuckle as they float by.

Shooting stars wish for a green light,
Yet all they want is a good night's bite.
Galactic jokes lost in the void,
Tickling the universe, how we've enjoyed!

From asteroids, meteors dare,
In a space game of tag—beware!
Gravity's just a party crasher so rude,
But we'll keep dancing in this cosmic mood.

The Symmetry of Celestial Dreams

In moonlit realms where thoughts conspire,
Cosmic giggles spark wild desire.
Stars knitted cozy in a quilt of light,
Dancing and twirling through the night.

Comets wearing hats zooming past,
Sharing punchlines that stick like paste.
Planets prance in a heavenly ballet,
While black holes giggle, pulling dreams away.

Aliens read our minds with flair,
Finding recipes for cosmic air.
Lost in thought, we take flight,
Giggles echo through the endless night.

Dreams may scatter like stardust on breeze,
Yet laughter binds us, we joke with ease.
The cosmos beams with its silly charms,
As we lay cradled in the universe's arms.

Intergalactic Portals to the Self

Step through the wormhole, hear the boing,
Every leap echoes with laughter's song.
Alien wisdom at quirky stalls,
Offering life advice with cosmic calls.

The universe swirls like a merry-go-round,
Slipping through paradox to be sound.
Zany reflections in star-lit pools,
Making us ponder, are we the fools?

A peek inside with goggles of humor,
Exoplanet parties, oh what a rumor!
Ego tickled by astrophysical jest,
Finding my center, amused but blessed.

Spacesuits shimmering with disco flair,
Twisting and twirling through midnight air.
Each galaxy a riddle, bursting with cheer,
In this endless voyage, nothing to fear.

Shadows of Distant Suns

In the night sky so sublime,
A pizza slice made of time.
Stars twinkle, doing a jig,
While aliens dance, just a bit big.

Shooting stars grab a snack,
On comets they'll never turn back.
The moon shrugs, a lazy chap,
While planets giggle in their map.

Lightyears away, they toast to fate,
With rock juice, they celebrate.
Each bright orb cracks a grin,
Saying, 'Let the fun begin!'

Celestial Cartography

Maps in space, all askew,
Drawn by quirky banjo crew.
Orion's belt, just a hunch,
Held together by a cosmic brunch.

Galaxies mix like odd cocktails,
Sipping light-speed without fails.
The Milky Way's a foam of cream,
In this map, it's all a dream.

Planets chat with big grins wide,
'Where to next?' they will bide.
With a wink, they zoom along,
Singing their own cosmic song.

The Rhythm of Cosmic Cycles

Planets whirl in a velvet dance,
Each spin a cosmic chance.
Jupiter leads with a big old twirl,
While Saturn spins with rings to unfurl.

Asteroids hop, all in a line,
Playing tag, oh so fine.
Halley's Comet bursts with glee,
When it's time for a cosmic tea.

Time ticks in a rhythm absurd,
As star stuff sings every word.
In the groove of space's fate,
They all just seem to celebrate.

Constellations of the Mind

Thoughts sparkle like stars afar,
Wishing on wishes, oh what bizarre!
Constellations make a silly face,
Drawing laughter in empty space.

Dreams collide in a bright balloon,
Floating high under a chuckling moon.
Ideas whirl like a waltz on high,
Tickling neurons as they fly.

Galactic giggles echo through time,
With every riddle and every rhyme.
In this vast expanse of cheer,
The cosmos whispers, 'Have no fear!'

Cosmic Callings

In the depths of space, a star sneezes loud,
A comet goes flying, oh look, what a crowd!
Aliens chuckle, they dance and they twirl,
'We're just looking for snacks,' they say with a whirl.

A planet spins slowly, feels a bit shy,
As black holes spin stories, they swirl and they cry.
Asteroids hurry, they know they must race,
For dinner's quite close, in this vast cosmic space.

Supernova sneezes, with glitter and flair,
While stars do the cha-cha with nary a care.
The universe giggles, all around us it bounces,
We're just little beings, on where humor pounces.

Galaxies laugh as they twirl in a show,
With neutron stars juggling, come and see the glow!
And as we float by, we can't help but grin,
Life's cosmic hilarity, let the fun times begin.

Journey through the Void

Floating through space in a big rubber tire,
Chasing strange dreams, with a laugh and some fire.
Planets wave hello, as we zoom on by,
While distant suns wink as they blink in the sky.

UFOs go karting, high-speed on a trail,
With Martians all giggling as they buy some gelato.
Asteroids are dodging, like kids in a game,
'No bumping!' they shout, 'Or it's all just the same!'

Black holes toss tickets to the cosmic fair,
While comets hold hands with the stardust in air.
Traveling through dark, we blast off in cheer,
For what's waiting ahead? A galactic frontier!

In the dance of the void, we twirl and we spin,
As laughter and stardust mix, that's where we begin.
Each moment a treasure, each giggle a note,
On our silly journey, forever we float!

Echoes of Existence

In the silence of space, a whisper goes wide,
A moon sings to planets, with no place to hide.
'Are we cosmic jokes?' asks the comet with flair,
As the universe chuckles, 'Oh darling, beware.'

Echoing laughter, through nebulae bright,
While stars spill confetti, oh what a delight!
'This life is a party, with cake made of dust,'
Said Saturn's fine rings, 'Now soar with us, must!'

Galactic giggles burst forth in delight,
With asteroid parties that last through the night.
Each supernova's pop, a balloon gone so loud,
While quasars do stand-up, a quirky space crowd!

Every echo a tale, spun light-years away,
Where comets and stardust all come out to play.
In the hush of the cosmos, we bumble and frolic,
Existence is funny, and oh so symbolic!

Galaxies of Meaning

In the swirl of the cosmos, meanings collide,
With black holes and giggles, laughter can't hide.
Stars throw confetti from their twinkling eyes,
While gravity teases with playful goodbyes.

Nebulae whisper their colorful secrets,
While pulsars spin yarns, with celestial regrets.
Hey Martians, they wave, come join in the fun,
As they juggle the moonbeams, one by one!

The Milky Way's banquet offers joy on a plate,
With meteor showers served fresh from the fate.
We raise a toast here, to our space-age delight,
Sharing cosmic chuckles beneath the starlit night!

And if you're feeling lost in this galactic spree,
Just follow the laughter, it will set you free.
For meaning's a puzzle that dances and glows,
In the heart of the universe, where humor flows!

Navigating the Cosmic Sea

In a ship made of cheese, we set to roam,
With stars as our compass, we're far from home.
The Milky Way's sprinkles, on toasted bread,
We laugh with the aliens, who dance in our head.

Galactic hiccups make our journey grand,
A comet that's sneezing, we just can't stand!
But with laughter as fuel, we soar through the void,
Navigating space, our fates are overjoyed.

Jellybean planets spin in delight,
While cosmonauts juggle meteors at night.
Space-time laughs echo in colorful hues,
As we float on fine waffles with maple syrup views.

With cosmic maps drawn in crayon and glue,
We chart out our course with a helium crew.
The secrets of the universe tickle our ears,
With a cosmic giggle, we've conquered our fears.

A Voyage Beyond Time

In a time machine wedged in my toaster,
I sailed through the ages, a real hipster poster.
With toast in my hand and jam on my face,
Each tick of the clock, I relish the chase.

I met dinosaurs dressed in their Sunday best,
While Shakespeare tried rapping, he's quite like the rest.
A selfie with Newton, all caught in a whirl,
His apple's gone wild; it could start a new swirl.

Riding the waves of a temporal tide,
I tumbled through centuries, no need to hide.
With laughter and scones, we danced through the past,
In a delightful mix-up, oh what a blast!

Now back in my kitchen, the toast burns away,
But the nuggets of wisdom will always stay.
For in every tick, there's a joke to be told,
In the great cosmic scheme, we're all pure gold!

Radiance of the Unknown

With glittering stardust stuck in my hair,
I skipped through the cosmos without a care.
I tripped on a black hole, but what a fun ride!
The laughter of planets just can't be denied.

A supernova's salsa caught my two left feet,
While aliens giggled and offered me a seat.
I googled the meaning of life on the spot,
But all I found was a joke—well, is that all I got?

They dressed me in lasers that sparkled and swirled,
As I danced with the comets, my mind gets twirled.
Galaxies wink with a flamboyant flair,
While I try to count all the tarantulas there.

The unknown is blushing in colors so bright,
As I twirl with the cosmos, oh what a sight!
In this cosmic charade, hilarity reigns,
For we laugh with the universe in its funny refrains.

Aligning with Celestial Truths

In cosmic yoga, I stretch towards the stars,
With my mat on a meteor, oh, how bizarre!
The sun's rays are smiles, the moon gives me winks,
As I strike my best pose, the galaxy blinks.

Planets line up, what a splendid parade,
While aliens throw confetti; we laugh unafraid.
A cosmic chant echoes, with rhythm and beat,
As we sway to the music, in zero-gravity heat.

Who knew the Milky Way rolled with such flair?
Its swirl is a dance move, beyond compare.
With laughter aligning the stars in my heart,
In this quirky ballet, we all play a part.

So I float with the stars, in this comical truth,
With the universe chuckling, reclaiming my youth.
From stardust to belly laughs, it's all intertwined,
For in this cosmic giggle, we're blissfully aligned.

Dreams Carved in Galactic Dust

In the vastness, dreams do dance,
Like socks lost in a cosmic chance.
Stars giggle with a twinkling cheer,
While planets spin, drinking space beer.

Aliens chuckle in their green suits,
Juggling comets, wearing space boots.
What a sight, the universe' quirk,
With every joke, the stars just smirk.

Galactic hiccups, a black hole's laugh,
All of us stuck in this cosmic graph.
Yet amidst the chaos, joy ignites,
In this dance with stardust on starry nights.

So let your dreams climb high and wide,
In the universe, let humor be your guide.
For every trip feels lighter, more fun,
When you laugh with galaxies, one by one.

The Light That Guides Unseen Paths

Through shadowed trails where starlight plays,
We stumble 'round in comical ways.
A guiding glow, we think we see,
Is just a firefly, sipping iced tea.

With every spark that lights our way,
We wander off, in bright disarray.
Navigating by a meteor's tail,
Is like following a fishy trail.

Fiddling with maps, our compass spins,
Seeking laughter as the greatest wins.
In a universe where jokes unfold,
Even dark matter can be quite bold.

So when in doubt, just tip your hat,
To cosmic wonders, and the silly spat.
For where we wander, the light will find,
Every chuckle's path, perfectly aligned.

Constellations of Our Heart's Desire

Stars draw pictures in the night air,
But can't sketch out just how we care.
Ursa Major's dance is quite a treat,
Yet she spills her popcorn, oh what a feat!

Orion's belt, so tightly spun,
Looks just like my laundry, all but done.
With wishes tossed to the Milky Way,
Our laughter echoes, then drifts away.

We aim for love with telescope eyes,
But end up lost in our own goodbyes.
Each orbit spins a fumble or two,
As comets comet their way right through.

Still in this tangent, let's shout and cheer,
For every miss leads us closer, dear.
In every star, a giggle we find,
As constellations weave, always intertwined.

Resonance of the Soul's Journey

In the echoes of space, we twirl and spin,
Passenger seats for laughter within.
Shooting stars off on wild retreats,
Trading jokes with black holes, oh what feats!

Through cosmic waves, we dance and sway,
In rhythm with giggles, come what may.
Each heartbeat resonates with sounds so bright,
When we collide, oh what a sight!

Journey's a ride on this whimsical train,
With laughter as fuel, through joy, not pain.
As we glide through galaxies so wide,
Let humor steer you, let it be your guide.

For in the end, it's all a big joke,
From the big bang to the cosmic yolk.
So hang on tight, enjoy the jest,
For the journey's the punchline, and laughter's the best!

Stars as Compasses of the Heart

When stars above light up the night,
I squint and think, is that my flight?
A compass made of twinkling lights,
Guiding me to mischief and bites.

The moon is just a giant pie,
With cosmic sprinkles piled high.
I'd take a slice if it weren't far,
Instead, I'll munch on this candy bar.

Comets zoom with blazing tails,
Telling tales of interstellar gales.
But all I want is a snack on earth,
What's the cosmic value of this mirth?

So if you gaze at heaven's dance,
And find my fortune, take a chance.
Join me in laughter, let's all play,
In this grand universe, hip-hip-hooray!

The Celestial Blueprint of Being

In the sky hangs a cosmic map,
Showing us life's intended slap.
With dots and lines, it all seems clear,
Except when Jupiter buys a beer.

Galaxies spin, what a crazy sight,
They twirl around; it's quite the fright.
But in this mess of stars and dust,
We find our joy, as we must.

Planets joke about their orbits tight,
"Hey! I'm the fastest, check my flight!"
But truth be told, it's all a game,
Just cosmic buddies, none feel shame.

So here's to all that's strange and odd,
The universe is just a bit flawed.
Yet in this chaos, laughter rings,
As we embrace the joy it brings!

When Galaxies Align: A Guiding Light

When galaxies align, I start to grin,
Thinking of Chaos as my twin.
Stars give wishes and flats of fate,
Yet here I am—still very late.

Constellations dance their silly jig,
I trip over stars, can you dig?
They laugh at me with milky grins,
"Keep dreaming dreams, where chaos begins!"

Gravity's pull is one big hug,
But I'm the shell stuck in a rug.
Floating through space, what a fantastic ride,
With a good old friend who's full of pride.

So when the cosmos plays its part,
Remember laughter's a stellar art.
For in the vastness, we find delight,
With cosmic giggles that shine so bright!

Reflections in the Cosmic Mirror

In the cosmic mirror, what do I see?
A wild-haired comet, that's surely me!
With galaxies swirling like hair in a mess,
I should really practice some space etiquette.

Nebulas burst, a paint-splattered scheme,
I wink at a wormhole, "What's your dream?"
It bends light like spacetime's great prank,
"Let's swap places, you should thank!"

Black holes giggle, "We're in the right,"
"Just suck up the fun, hold on tight!"
While stars chuckle, "Hey, that's our light!"
Creating a show that's quite the fright.

A cosmic giggle from this crazy sphere,
Whispers, "Life's a ride, so hold it dear."
Here's to laughs across the night sky,
In this wild universe, let's reach for the high!

Entwined in Cosmic Lace

In the vastness where comets dance,
The aliens giggle at their own chance.
A noodle-shaped star, with ketchup in tow,
Spaghetti meetings? They put on a show!

Asteroids play tag, quite the ruckus,
While Martian cats chase their cosmic buses.
And what of the moons? They love to broil,
In a frying pan sun, they shimmer and coil!

Black holes serve snacks, but they suck in the fun,
"Hey, don't eat my chips!" shouts a quasar on the run.
With laughter so bright, they sprinkle their cheer,
In a universe quirky, full of folks so dear!

So twirl with the stars, let laughter ignite,
For even in space, we find pure delight.
Each giggle a comet, each chuckle a ray,
In this cosmic dance, we laugh all the way!

The Alchemy of Starlight

Two stars in a bar, swapping old jokes,
While Neptune serves drinks, and Mars makes some smokes.
They mix up a potion of giggles and darts,
Creating new comets and cosmic funny parts!

"Why did the star break up?" asks one with a grin,
"Because it needed more space, let the fun begin!"
The light-years between them, they laugh and they glee,
In this great cosmic pub, just happy to be free!

Galaxies spin, in a wobbly swirl,
While asteroids dance in a cosmic twirl.
The universe chuckles, with stardust in its mane,
In the alchemy of light, there's never a strain!

Let's toast to the black holes, rich in despair,
For they're always the life of the party, I swear!
With moons like disco balls and comets that sing,
In the alchemy of joy, we all are the bling!

Veils of Cosmic Lore

In a nebula café, where dreams take a seat,
A saturnian waitress serves some cosmic treat.
With tales of the galaxies and planets afar,
She tells us of bacon made out of stars!

"Did you hear about Pluto? Got kicked out of the game!"
"Oh that poor little planet, what a wild claim!"
The stars all chime in, with giggles and sighs,
For even in space, there's laughter that flies!

With meteors racing, and quarks in a fuss,
The secrets of space make the cosmos a plus.
A comedy cosmic, where black holes compose,
The funny little stories that nobody knows.

So gather your friends, and don't be a bore,
Let's weave through the galaxies, laughing galore!
In the veils of the cosmos, we write our own lore,
With quirks and with chuckles, who could ask for more?

The Melodies of the Milky Way

In the band of the cosmos, juiced up with zeal,
Stars strum the guitars, making light how they feel.
A supernova solo, with drums made of dust,
In the melodies swirling, we dance and we trust!

A comet on saxophone, smooth with its curves,
While Venus keeps time, with cosmic observes.
"Hey Earth! You missed the beat!" Mocks a nearby quark,

While black holes spin tales, deep into the dark.

Shooting stars whistle, with every bright dash,
While planets on keyboards create quite the clash.
The universe hums, with a symphony grand,
Full of quirky notes, from this stellar band!

So grab a few meteors, dance under the night,
With the melodies cosmic, we're lost in delight.
From Saturn's sweet rings to the suns' fiery rays,
In the grand cosmic concert, let's sing all our praise!

Celestial Harmonies of the Heart

In a galaxy of quirks, we twirl,
With comets and donuts, let laughter swirl.
Stars wink at us with silly glee,
We dance in the light of our cosmic spree.

Planets giggle, spinning in jest,
While meteors prance, they're feeling blessed.
Each twinkle sings a tune of the night,
In this infinite circus, it feels so right.

Asteroids shout, 'Hey! Catch me if you can!'
While black holes laugh at their own grand plan.
Galaxy maps drawn in crayon bright,
Navigating life with pure delight.

So let's toast to the void, it's a marvelous sight,
With a wink and a grin, we'll take flight!
In stardust and chuckles, we find our way,
Embracing the chaos, come what may!

The Universe's Gentle Nudge

A star sneezed and sent us a quirk,
Sending space debris with a smirk.
Galaxies giggle, tumbling amiss,
A gentle nudge turned into bliss.

Planets align for a cosmic dance,
Each orbit jests, as if by chance.
Pulsars pulse with a comedic beat,
In this universe, life's a treat!

Black holes whisper, 'Just let it be!'
As time ticks away in a tea party spree.
Gravity pulls us closer, what a game,
In the realm of the wacky, never the same.

So let's ride the waves of this silly plan,
With laughter echoing from star to span.
For in the vastness, we're never alone,
With each joke of the cosmos, we've truly grown!

Woven Destinies Among the Stars

In the fabric of space, threads intertwine,
Woven by giggles, a cosmic design.
Each planet a stitch, each star a line,
Creating a quilt, oh so divine.

Nebulas craft clouds of bright chaff,
While supernovae erupt with a laugh.
We stitch our dreams in the cosmic loom,
Beneath the vast sky, we dance and zoom.

Galactic yarns spun with glee,
Entangled destinies, just you and me.
Spaghetti of stars in the night's embrace,
Woven together in a playful space.

So grab your needle, let's sew our fate,
With laughter as glue, it's never too late.
In the tapestry grand, we twirl and sway,
Finding joy in this chaotic ballet!

Cosmic Seeds of Resolve

In the garden of stars, we plant our dreams,
Watered by giggles and cosmic beams.
Tiny seeds sprout with a wink and a cheer,
Growing in laughter, with naught a fear.

Asteroids roll like playful pups,
While moons perform acrobatic jumps.
Each little spark, a quirky belief,
Woven together, in joy, not grief.

Galaxies chat, sharing silly plans,
While suns spread warmth to all distant lands.
Comets dash by with a whoosh and a grin,
In this great expanse, we all fit in.

So let's cultivate joy in the stellar field,
With cosmic resolve, our hearts will yield.
In the vastness of night, we'll plant our cheer,
Spreading love like stardust, year after year!

In the Shadow of Giants

Beneath the toes of giants, we play,
Chasing our dreams, come what may.
They stomp and they laugh, it's quite a show,
Yet we giggle and dodge, just trying to grow.

With lunch bags filled with hope and crumbs,
We overtake the feet, avoid their drums.
Oh, to be big, to rule the land,
But we lose the chase, due to a stray hand!

In shadows cast from towering heights,
We build our forts and have our fights.
Tiny armies made of peas and cheese,
Conquerors of snack time, oh what a breeze!

So here we are, in this great charade,
With giants above, our plans still laid.
We'll dance and we'll jump, till the sun goes down,
In this funny arena, we wear the crown.

The Light We Seek

In search of the glow that tickles the mind,
We gather our lanterns, and off we unwind.
Chasing the sparkle, our feet get all sore,
Tripping on shadows, oh what a bore!

Yet still we laugh, with grace and with flair,
As we twirl around, without a single care.
What is this light? A cupcake? A star?
Or just a reflection of our wild car?

We peek under bushes, and dash up the trees,
In hopes to discover a slice of the cheese.
The light flickers on, it's a firefly's glow,
Given to us, for the fun of the show!

So let's raise our cups to the glow in the night,
The laughter we share, what a delightful sight.
With fireflies twirling, we all take a leap,
In this dance of the light, our happiness keeps!

The Abyss of Our Dreams

In the depths of our dreams, where silliness thrives,
We ride on wild llamas, and play with our lives.
Swirling in marshmallows, taking a dip,
In search of that jelly, oh what a trip!

We float through the void with a wink and a grin,
Chasing the thoughts that make our heads spin.
Sailing on cupcakes, we're off to the seas,
With jellybean anchors, we ride the breeze!

Oh puffy clouds, they're our trusted crew,
As we scream, "To the abyss!" with a laugh or two.
Knowing that dreamland is oddly absurd,
Like wearing a hamster as a funny bird.

So let's jump right in, invite all our friends,
To the abyss where imagination never ends.
With giggles and chaos, we'll navigate through,
In this land of the wacky, where dreams come true!

Beneath the Celestial Canopy

Beneath the stars, we lay in a line,
Counting the twinkles like they're ours to dine.
Trading our wishes for giggles and grins,
In this cosmic circus, let the fun begin!

The moon winks at us, with a fruity cheer,
As we ponder life's questions, while sipping on beer.
What if the sun was just a big light bulb?
Or Saturn's rings were some fashionable glob?

So dance with the comets, they love a good jam,
Twirling and diving, our intergalactic slam.
With laughter as fuel, we'll soar through the night,
In this silly universe, everything feels right!

So here's to the sky, with its playful embrace,
And the dreams that we dream, as we leave our trace.
For beneath this bright canvas, we live and we play,
In a cosmic adventure that's true every day!

Unlocking the Mysteries of the Sky

Where did all the aliens hide?
I think they're under my bed, side by side.
They play cards with shadows and giggle so low,
Plotting to steal my last piece of dough.

Stars twinkle like they know a big secret,
But all they whisper is about the next comet.
They send me postcards from across the night,
Yet all I find is a meteor bite.

Space cats float on cosmic beams,
Chasing nachos and endless dreams.
They meow in riddles, oh what a sight,
While I just wonder if I'll sleep tonight.

So here I sit with my nose pressed to glass,
Imagining aliens hosting a cosmic class.
They'd teach me to dance on a solar flare,
And laugh at gravity's continual glare.

A Journey Through Cosmic Whisperings

I asked a galaxy for some good advice,
It said to order pizza, but hold the spice!
Asteroids flew by to give me a hand,
While meteors laughed at my not-so-grand plan.

I wore a tutu made of starry threads,
Doing the moonwalk while my dog treads.
Planets rolled by, they couldn't believe,
That classic bad dance moves could achieve.

Neptune shook its head, Jupiter rolled its eyes,
Said, "Dancing's not for us, we just rise!"
But out there in the cold, I spun like a top,
With black holes cheering, "Don't ever stop!"

A comet waved and flipped me the bird,
"Join the infinity line, haven't you heard?"
So I floated on dreams, to the edge of the sway,
Where cosmic giggles keep worries at bay.

Threads of Stardust and Letting Go

In a sock drawer of space, I found something grand,
A sock from a comet, the yellow one's banned!
They say it can grant you a galactic wish,
But I just wanted a really nice dish.

I wrote my dreams on a little bright star,
A wish to be rich, or a rock-n-roll czar.
But it flipped my note, and laughed in my face,
Turning my dreams into a funny disgrace.

Galaxies giggled, "What a naïve child!"
While I painted nebulas, feeling quite wild.
With each brushstroke, I let my dreams flow,
Creating a masterpiece of glitter and glow.

Then I spilled my tea, and sent it to Mars,
As the planets all whimpered, "Don't play with our jars!"
So I cleaned up the cosmos, in my own funky way,
And turned all my blunders into a ballet.

The Cosmic Veil of Wonder

Behind the curtain, twins suns play peek-a-boo,
While space dust dances, like it always knew.
I whisper my secrets to a black hole's ear,
But it just swallows them, like yesterday's beer.

I tried to count planets, got lost in the mix,
As comets crashed parties with shiny, wild tricks.
Mars baked cookies that tasted like dirt,
"Just a sprinkle of stardust!" it said with a flirt.

I rode on a meteor, what a wild ride,
Through belts of rocks where the space lizards hide.
They wore hats and glasses, all so absurd,
Discussing their dinner, the tastiest bird.

So here's to the cosmos, a playful grand scene,
Where laughter and wonder reigns supreme.
When life feels too serious, just look to the sky,
For the universe winks and gives a good try!

Patterns in the Void

In the dark, stars twinkle bright,
Like disco balls, oh what a sight!
Space dust dances like it's shy,
While aliens giggle, oh my, oh my!

Comets race with playful glee,
As meteorites sip cosmic tea.
A black hole's laugh, a silly swirl,
Swallowing planets in a twirl!

Galaxies spin in a wacky tune,
Space squirrels scurrying by the moon.
Asteroids in a conga line,
Joking with planets to sip on wine!

But here we are, earthbound and meek,
Looking for meaning week after week.
Yet, in this void, lighthearted and gay,
Laughter's a compass that shows us the way!

The Map Beneath the Stars

With a map written in stardust ink,
I wander 'neath the cosmic pink.
Finding X where the silly sun shines,
That marks the treasure of pizza vines!

Voyagers float with a quirky grin,
Hitching rides on comets, oh what a win!
They point to Mars, 'That's the place!',
But find only Martians eating space cake!

Navigating through this galactic maze,
Where everyone's lost in their own funny phase.
I ask the moon, 'What's the best route?'
He chuckles back, 'Take the path with a pout!'

Yet as we laugh, the night unfolds,
Mapping the stars that we haven't sold.
Maybe getting lost is just a fun part,
Of finding our way with a light-hearted heart!

Embracing the Cosmic Calling

In the vastness, a voice I hear,
It says, 'Dance, don't you fear!'
So I twirl with joy, like a spinning top,
In this grand cosmos, I can't stop!

Lasers beam in a cheery shade,
Space whales singing in a masquerade.
They lift my spirit, make me sway,
With giggles echoing in a playful display!

Planets popping popcorn, what a sight!
Stardust showers, a delight!
Cosmic beings tease with a wink,
'Join the fun, come have a drink!'

So here I am, floating and free,
Embracing this crazy cosmic spree.
Amid the stars, I find my song,
With laughter and joy, I'll dance along!

Echoes of Existence: A Celestial Tale

Once upon a time, in a galaxy far,
Lived a cat on a comet, chasing a star.
With paws so light, and a swish of a tail,
Creating chaos, a cosmic trail!

Echoes of laughter met starlight's tune,
A duck floated by, playing the moon.
Together they schemed, what a pair!
Grabbing saturn's rings for a cosmic fair!

As aliens danced 'round a neon sun,
I wondered, 'Is this really all just for fun?'
Yet they shared tales of laughter and fright,
As the black hole guffawed into the night!

So if you listen in starry nights,
You might catch whispers of cosmic delights.
For through the universe, laughter prevails,
In echoes of existence, we weave our tales!

www.ingramcontent.com/pod-product-compliance
Lightning Source LLC
Chambersburg PA
CBHW071850160426
43209CB00003B/495